She had a dream.

He had a pursuit.

He smiled, she smiled.

He helped, she complied.

Eventually, every night before she went to sleep, he asked her for three words so he could conjure up a bedtime story and always started it with "Once Upon a Time..."

In the 50 days before his 50th birthday, she decided to tell him more than three words everyday to sum up how she felt about him.

On the 360th day of their time together, he died.

Within 50 seconds of finding these notes along with the many objects she saved of his, she wrote a refrain in her sorrow.

This is a love story

Anyone's love story.

ONCE UPON A TIME.

before...

Day 50

"You brighten the darkest nights."

Day 50
You brighten
The darkest
nights.

& after

> You brightened the darkest nights and made me love who I was.

HOPE.

before...

Day 49

"You are NICE & naughty."

& after

You were nice & naughty, your arm around me as we spooned, your hand on my...

PASSION.

before...

Day 48

"You are curious like George."

& after

You were curious like George in
the way you took apart things
to see how they worked.

CURIOUS.

before...

Day 47

"You say pahtahto, I say potatoe."

& after

I said tomato,
you said tomahto,
but we didn't
call it off.

UNIQUE.

before...

Day 46

"You have the best sense of humor and can create a smile on someone instantly."

& after

You had the best ways to diffuse, distract and just be yourself at any given moment to bring ease into the room.

FUNNY.

before...

Day 45

"You love the moon & stars, too!"

& after

You loved the moon &
being in its light with love...
we watched the most awesome
moon in LBK quietly embraced.

UNIVERSE.

before...

Day 44

"A true gentle man."
(Your Mum would be proud.)

& after

You called me young lady and carried more for me than you will ever know.

REAL.

before...

Day 43

"You live life authentically."

& after

You lived life on your terms,
realizing what you truly needed.

AUTHENTIC.

before...

Day 42

"Imagination is everything.
It is the preview of life's coming attractions."

~ Albert Einstein

& after

Once Upon a Time...

Your bedtime stories were the best.

SMILE.

before...

Day 41

"In you, a wish came true."

& after

A wish did come true... in you.

WISH.

before...

Day 40

"I love the way you say my name."

& after

DEBBIE, Debbie, debbie

VOICE.

before...

Day 39

"Com-pas-sion-ate, adjective,
Definition: Simon"

& after

You redefined the word compassion in the way your eyes welled up with mine.

YOU.

before...

Day 38

"You see life in a unique way, that is what makes you a great photographer."

& after

I liked the way you taught me to fine-tune an image because it meant we could be close.

SKYLINE.

before...

Day 37

"You have an undeniable youthful spirit that is oh-so contagious."

& after

You found my weak giggle spot more than once.

ROMANTIC.

before...

Day 36

"You are going in the direction
of your dream."

& after

It took me a while to realize the dream really included me.

DREAMS.

before...

Day 35

"Your eyes twinkle with mischievousness, SIMON!"

& after

Your nose wrinkled up too
when you found something
really funny.
(I noticed daily)

SENSUAL.

before...

Day 34

"You are able to scale
large mountains."

& after

Taking me to the top of the mountain on my birthday was a high point in my life.

EXPLORE.

before...

Day 33

"We go perfectly hand-in-hand with each other."

& after

I miss those hands on my thigh,
my face, my waist...

WE.

before...

Day 32

"You know how to stoke a fire."

& after

Literally in a fire pit and figuratively within me.

CANDLE.

before...

Day 31

"Nothing compares to the simple pleasure of a bike ride."

"Ride on Simon!"

July 19, 2018

& after

Potato chips shared as we rode
our bikes along the rail trail,
like two teenagers.

RIDE.

before...

Day 30

"I LOVE you, I LOVE us."

Perpetly interchained

& after

Perfectly intertwined—
a love team.

LOVE.

before...

Day 29

"Your hand resting on me has
the ability to calm me
in an instant."

& after

I loved calming you as I stroked your hair and held you close.

CALM.

before...

Day 28

"You have embraced life
more than anyone I know."

& after

Living in the moment with you
is why I can remember
everything about you.

LIFE.

before...

Day 27

"My favorite place with you is being entangled with you."

& after

And despite our difference in height, we could entangle like no other.

PLACES.

before...

Day 26

"You are intuitive, instinctive & full of wonderfulness."

Day 24
You are intuitive, instinctive + full of wonderfulness.
♥ xo ɒɒ.

& after

You always knew when a hug was needed either by text or in real-time.

INTUITIVE.

before...

Day 25

"Your generosity
is beyond words."

& after

Your Christmas gift to me—an updated powder room—was more than awesome.

GENEROUS.

before...

Day 24

"You are a beacon of light followed by love. "

& after

You flickered and I caught the fire. The moment you told me at the right moment I needed a hug.

LIGHT.

before...

Day 23

"Life is just beginning at 50."

& after

I am forever grateful I helped you usher in this milestone birthday.

JOY.

before...

Day 22

"Bunbury's true super hero."

& after

You made me realize I could not do this all alone and that your help (in more ways than one) was given at the right time.

DIFFERENCE.

before...

Day 21

"My heart is grateful everyday
for your new beats."

& after

I met you.

GRATEFUL.

before...

Day 20

"You have a humble, gentle and beautiful way to encourage others."

& after

You inspired so many—
I hope you knew.

HUMBLE.

before...

Day 19

"You are full of childhood wonderment."

& after

A ramble in nature to catch the melting snow—perfect for making snow people.

FREE.

before...

Day 18

"You go above and beyond in all that you do."

& after

Always stopping what you may be doing to lend a hand.

DO.

before...

Day 17

"For your optimistic view on embracing life the way it should be lived."

& after

A gift—'Never A Bad Day' mug
that sums up your outlook
on all.

EMBRACE.

before...

Day 16

"You just make everything taste better."

& after

Your ability to concoct a meal
in a creative way.

TASTY.

before...

Day 15

"Always a step ahead
to keep others safe—
beautiful walking with you."

& after

The way you lit the bike path in
LBK with your phone light so
I could follow you closely.

SAFE.

before...

Day 14

"You are always up for an adventure."

& after

What an adventure we had.

ADVENTUROUS.

before...

Day 13

"The way you make me feel
when we are alone."

& after

When we were alone,
I wasn't lonely.

FEELINGS.

before…

Day 12

"Your commitment to date night."

& after

The time you were at my house—already—and as I got ready for date night, you left and then returned in 60 seconds, rang the doorbell and asked me out.

COMMITMENT.

before...

Day 11

"On 11/11 lucky numbers and
a year for you SIMON.
(I am (HEART) lucky, too)"

& after

Borrowed time.

LUCKY.

before...

Day 10

"You know how to fix things...
especially my heart."

& after

The moment you said you could fix "that" something in the shop, you already had.

TRUST.

before...

Day 9

"It just takes 10 seconds to
refill my heart
when I see & touch you."

& after

10, 9 ¾, 9 ½, 9 ¼, 9, 8 & so on,
and so on, and so on…
to overfill.

SWEET.

before...

Day 8

"You have the perfect nook between your head and shoulder to snuggle in."

& after

Whenever you asked...
my answer always was to blend
with you the closest way
possible.

LOVE-LY.

before...

Day 7

"Your attention to detail,
polishing as you go...
especially a rusty little
heart as mine was."

& after

Unbeknownst to both of us—
just moments before life
would forever change—
you asked me if I had what
I needed.

ATTENTIVE.

before...

Day 6

"The little things you do so naturally,
like putting toothpaste
on my toothbrush."

& after

It was little and huge at the same time.

CARING.

before...

Day 5

"I adore, love and appreciate the wonderful soul you are."

& after

The day I whispered,
"I adore you" in front of the
shop, in front of so many people
after you made the Bunbury's
flag for the bike rack.
You turned red, I fled.

ADORE.

before...

Day 4

"The Universe has beautiful plans—
make a wish."

& after

Maybe I will know someday
of those plans.

WISHES.

before...

Day 3

"You light up my life."

& after

> Sometimes, when I was with you, I purposely put the light on at night to prove you weren't just a dream next to me.

BEACON.

before...

Day 2

"You make me want to be
a better person."
(I love even those things you
dislike in you!)

& after

You were patient with my words
and you communicated clearly.

INSPIRATIONAL.

before...

Day 1

"In theory... you will be 50,
but honestly, why count?"

& after

> Just a number, the heart is infinite in love.

THEORIST.

before...

Birthday.

Happy 50th Birthday!

(Because as someone once said everything will be alright in the end and if it's not alright then trust me, it's not yet the end.)

& after

Thank you, my love xoxo
Kindred Spirits & Souls
Connected.

(Parting with such sweet sorrow)

BITTERSWEET.

www.ingramcontent.com/pod-product-compliance
Lightning Source LLC
Chambersburg PA
CBHW071721020426
42333CB00017B/2353